Sharing

By Janine Amos and Annabel Spenceley
Consultant Rachael Underwood

A Cherrytree book

Designed and produced by
A S Publishing

First published 1997
by Cherrytree Press
327 High Street
Slough
Berkshire
SL1 1TX

First softcover edition 1999

Reprinted 2000

Copyright © Evans Brothers Limited 1997

British Library Cataloguing in Publication Data
Amos, Janine
       Sharing. - (Growing Up)
       1. Sharing - Juvenile literature
       1. Title
       302.1'4

       ISBN 1 84234 008 5

Printed in Malaysia

Ali and Sara

Ali is playing with all the playdough.

Sara wants to play too.

Sara grabs the dough.

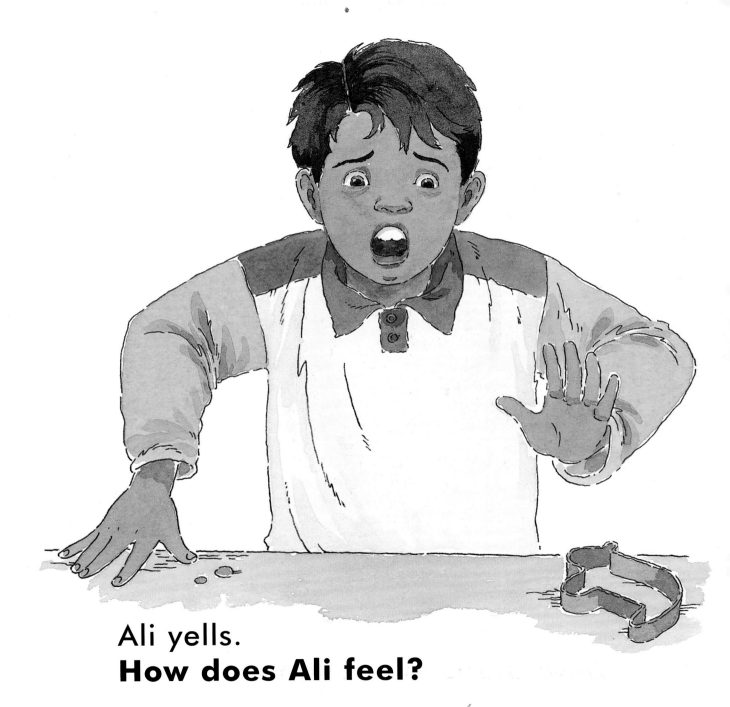

Ali yells.
How does Ali feel?

Dave comes to talk with them.

"What's going on?" he asks.

"I want the dough!" shouts Sara.

"I was using it!" screams Ali.

"Ali, you sound angry," says Dave.

"And, Sara, you really want the playdough."

Sara and Ali nod.

"I need lots of dough to make my farm," says Ali.

"I need some to make a pizza,"
says Sara.

**Sara and Ali both want the dough.
What could they do?**

Sara thinks hard.

"Ali can give me some of the dough to make my pizza," she says. "He can have the rest."

Ali thinks about it.

He gives Sara one handful of dough.
Then he gives her some more.

"You've solved the problem. You
are sharing the dough," says Dave.

Alex and Kelly

Alex has some strawberries.

Kelly comes over.
"I want some," she says.

"Here," says Alex.

Kelly takes three strawberries.
"Hey!" says Alex. "That's too many!"

Kelly looks at the strawberries.
"I know!" she says.

What do you think Kelly will do?

Kelly gives Alex one of her strawberries.

Now they have two each.

Sometimes two people want the same thing.
But together they can work it out.

When you want something,
ask the other person.
Talk about what you both need.
Together find a way that will work
for both of you.